"The fact is that whether you eat or drink – whatever you do – you should do all for the glory of God."

1 Corinthians 10:31

Tin Cups & Tinder

A Catholic Boy's Little Book of Fire, Food & Fun

By Alice Cantrell
(With significant input from Noah, Caleb & Collin Cantrell)

Art With A Mission

Tin Cups & Tinder: A Catholic Boy's Little Book of Fire, Food & Fun
Copyright © 2010 Alice Cantrell

Acknowledgements:
Thanks (yet again) to Chip and all the kids for picking up the slack around the home that inevitably occurs when Mom is in the middle of a "project". And a special thank you to those cool "boy saints" whom I got to know so well during the writing of this little book.

Bio:
Alice is a Catholic wife and homeschooling mother of six lively blessings, living (and drawing, painting, making and writing) in beautiful south Louisiana.

Photo credits:
Noah Cantrell
Caleb Cantrell
Collin Cantrell

Also by Alice Cantrell:
Sewing With Saint Anne: A Sewing Book for Catholic Girls
Tea & Cake With The Saints: A Catholic Young Lady's Introduction to
    Hospitality and the Home Arts

ISBN: 1453791108
EAN-13: 9781453791103

Art With A Mission
Kaplan, Louisiana
www.alicecantrell.com

May the work of our hands give glory to our Creator!

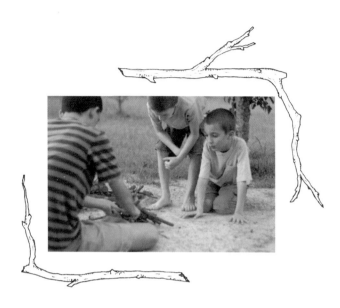

For my boys.

O Sacred Heart of Jesus,
I place my trust in Thee.

CONTENTS

A NOTE TO PARENTS

The purpose of this little book is to casually introduce a few domestic survival skills to our boys using useful recipes and other projects all lightly seasoned with the rich flavors of our Faith. It is not meant to be a home economics text, but a first taste of what fun adventures cooking and (very) basic stitching can be. It is my hope that this book will spark an interest in these things, and as they get older, our boys might be more inclined to further develop these skills.

Most of the recipes and projects included here are quite simple, but for the younger child, parental assistance will be necessary. Believe it or not, for most kids, doing these things with Mom or Dad makes them all the more fun!

WARNING: Please supervise your children when they are using fire, pocket knives or are working in the kitchen. All of the projects, recipes and suggestions in this book are written under the assumption that the boy doing the activity is properly supervised with a parent or older sibling standing by ready to offer his or her help and guidance.

"I will instruct you and teach you in the way you should go;
I will counsel you and watch over you."
Psalm 32:8

IMPORTANT!

Do not attempt any of the projects in this book involving cooking (inside or out), fire or knives without the permission of your parents!

(Oh yes, and any *italicized* words you come across are
most likely defined in the Glossary on page 104. Have fun!)

St. Lawrence of Rome
patron saint of cooks and chefs,
pray for us!

St. John Bosco

St. John Bosco (also known as St. Don Bosco) was born in 1815 in a small cabin deep in the hills of northern Italy. He spent much of his youth as a shepherd helping to support his family after losing his father at the tender age of two. From very early in life John had a fervent desire to become a priest, and despite his work in the fields, he studied hard and was ordained in 1841.

It was not long into his priestly ministry in the city of Turin, Italy, when John began to become aware of the difficult lives many of the city's poor children were forced to live. He resolved to help the unfortunate young boys (and later the girls also) by first inviting them to come and learn the catechism on Sundays. Eventually he established a school, the Oratory of St Francis de Sales, to educate the poor children of the streets and to teach them about God.

John Bosco made education his vocation and life's work. Not only did he teach the young, but he also wrote many booklets and papers to help the simple, ordinary people to better learn their Catholic Faith. Because of his early and devout focus on helping the boys of Turin, St. John Bosco is a patron saint of *all* boys. So the next time you are struggling with a math test, or just trying to remember the capitol of Portugal, try asking him to help you out a bit. He loves helping boys now that he is in Heaven as much as he did on Earth. He will take your requests right to Our Lord.

St. John Bosco,
patron saint of boys,
pray for us!

KITCHENS INSIDE & OUT

"You know that while all the runners in the stadium take part in the race, the award goes to one man. In that case, run so as to win! Athletes deny themselves all sorts of things. They do this to win a crown of leaves that withers, but we a crown that is imperishable."

1 Corinthians 9:24-25

Getting Started in the Kitchen

There is nothing quite as satisfying as eating something that you have prepared and cooked yourself. Before diving into the kitchen, however, there are a few things that it helps to remember:

- Wash your hands! Clean hands (even under those finger nails) are extremely important when working with anything anyone will be eating or drinking.

- Protect your clothing with a good sturdy apron. Did you know that aprons were once only used by men? It's true! They have been used since Biblical times by men to protect their clothing, but it was only much later that women began to wear them.

- Read through an entire recipe before beginning.

- Gather all the tools and ingredients you will need before beginning. Don't forget the pot holders for removing hot pans from the oven. (For instructions on making some cool ones of your own, see page 65.)

- If you do not have much experience in the kitchen, you may want to ask a parent for help.

- Clean up after yourself! Do not leave a mess behind you when you work in the kitchen. Be careful to put things back in their place, wash any dishes and tools you used and wipe off the counter top and other food preparation surfaces. A great way to clean these areas is to fill a spray bottle with plain vinegar, spray it on and wipe it off with a clean cloth. Studies have shown that vinegar kills 99% of bacteria, 82% of mold and 80% of viruses. It makes a great simple and safe all-purpose cleaner. A sink filled with hot soapy water is convenient for dropping dirty dishes into and makes clean-up even easier.

And finally, *be safe!* When using sharp knives or vegetable peelers, *always* cut away from your hand, and make sure to keep pot handles on the stove top turned in so that they do not accidently get bumped into. Always protect your hands by using pot holders when removing pans from the oven.

All of the recipes in this book can be cooked in your kitchen, but many of them also work quite well cooked over an open fire! Those recipes which are particularly fire-friendly are marked with this little symbol: Read on to learn more about camp-fire cooking.

A Fire to Cook On

If you are going to cook over a fire, the most important thing to remember is that you do not want cook over *high* flames, but over a nice bed of coals (low flames will be ok for some things). If wood is scarce, you can also use the same charcoal that is used for barbeque grills.

Making the Fire:

When selecting and gathering wood for your fire, try to collect dry, smallish logs and branches about 3-4 inches in diameter or about the size of your arm. This size will burn down into coals quicker than larger logs. Don't forget to pick up plenty of small dry twigs for *kindling*. Before lighting your fire, gather enough wood (including tinder and kindling) to get your fire going well. This is especially important if it is getting dark because fuel for your fire will be difficult to find once the sun has set.

Now that you have a good supply of wood, look around for something to use for *tinder*. Ideas for tinder include: dried moss, pine needles, pine cones, litter or other paper, dried leaves, dried grass, thistle down or the fluff inside dried cattails (they are perfect for this in the fall). You can also use bits of cotton cloth and even dryer lint from non-synthetic fabrics. What you are looking for is something that will light easily, yet hold a flame long enough to let the kindling begin to burn.

Fire Making Terms to Know

Coals - The hot, glowing or smoldering fragments of wood or coal left from a fire.

Embers – Coals that have cooled down enough so that they have stopped glowing.

Kindling - Material for starting a fire, such as small sticks of dry wood used to help build the fire after the tinder is lit.

Tinder - Any dry, easily flammable material used for getting a fire started and lighting the kindling.

If you are not using an established fire ring or designated campfire area, you will need to clear the ground of all leaves and dry grass in an area 3 feet in diameter before building the fire. A fire for cooking over need not be very large; in fact smaller is actually better in that it will be easier to control. When building your fire, first start with the tinder at the base (**1**), and then place the then kindling (in the form of a tepee) over the tinder (**2**). A fire must have plenty of air circulation to burn, so arrange the kindling loose enough to allow air to flow freely and leave a bit of the tinder exposed for lighting.

Now, light your fire! The tinder should catch easily and the flames will then travel to the kindling. (If you are having difficulties lighting the tinder, consider making a supply of *firestarters* as found on page 20.) Once your fire is burning well, you will need to carefully add a few more of the larger logs (**3**) and then wait about a half an hour for a good bed of coals to develop. It is the brightly, or even softly, glowing coals that you are looking for. These will be the heat source that cooks your food.

If you have made a larger fire and would like to continue to enjoy a nice blaze while you cook, simply use a shovel or hoe to rake a pile of coals off to the side for cooking on. When you are finished with your fire, douse it with plenty of water, then stir the smoldering ashes and douse again.

Keep Your Tinder Dry

These were important words of wisdom back in the days when fire was vital for both warmth and meal preperation. "Keep your tinder dry" means not only to prevent moisture from making your tinder useless, but to be prepared and to plan ahead. The all important supply of dry tinder was kept on the hearth of the firplace in a water resistant box and even worn (in a smaller box or leather pouch) around a person's neck, under their clothing, when they were out on the trail or in the woods. By gathering and storing their nice dry tinder when they found it, they were always prepared for fire making time, even in damp weather.

If you would like to put together your own tinderbox, a small candy tin is a nice size to tuck into a backpack or even a pocket. As you come across materials that would make good tinder (see page 20 for ideas), chop or tear them into small pieces and store them in your tinderbox. A few of last year's used birthday candles are a terriffic addition to any tinderbox. These little candles hold a flame much longer than a match giving you more time to get the tinder and kindling lit. If you want to add matches to your tin, either use "strike anywhere" matches, or cut the strike panel from an empty box of matches and glue it to the exterior of the candy tin. An alternative to matches is a flint with a steel striker (in photo to left). It produces a spark that is over 5,000 degrees Fahrenheit and will even work when wet!

For a somewhat messy but easy to make (and long burning) *firestarter*, simply coat a regular sized cotton ball in petrolium jelly. About a dozen of these coated cotton balls will stuff neatly into a matchstick holder from the camping section of a department or sporting goods store, or any other small container.

An assortment of home-made and commercially available tinders:

1. **Thistle Down** (From thistle plants after they have gone to seed.)
2. **Birch Bark** (Take only what is peeling off anyway. Do not strip bark from tree!)
3. **Cotton Balls Coated in Petrolium Jelly**
4. **Fire Sticks** (Sold in camping supply stores.)
5. **Tinder Quick** (Sold in camping supply stores.)

Cooking on the Coals

The tools listed below are by no means essential – except perhaps the shovel – but they do make cooking over an open fire more enjoyable.

- A small shovel
- A foldable grill
- Cast iron or other sturdy pots
- Heavy duty aluminum foil
- Pot holders (See page 65 to make your own.)
- A Camp Dutch oven with lid lifter
- Cooking tripod

Once you have created a nice hot bed of coals with very little flame, you are ready to begin cooking. There are two distinct ways of cooking with coals or a low fire. The first is to cook right *in* the hot cinders and coals, and the second is to cook *over* them.

To cook directly in the coals, one can carefully place a cast iron skillet or pot on top of them or make an aluminum foil packet to place food into and then on the coals. One of the very best ways to bake on a cook fire is to use a special pot called a *"camp Dutch oven"*. These large cast iron pots have short legs to allow a nice nest of hot coals to sit underneath the Dutch oven. The lid has a lip or flange around the edge so that coals can be piled on top allowing the heat to come from above and below at the same time. This wonderful tool allows one to bake almost anything over an open fire. (See page 28 for more on cooking in a Dutch oven.)

To cook over the coals, a pot can be suspended from a *cooking tripod* or other sturdy framework, placed on a grill (a medium sized folding grill is very useful), or held over the heat on a long stick (Hot dogs are frequently cooked this way.).

Equivalent Measures Chart

The chart below will be useful if you are trying to halve, double or even triple a recipe. It is useful to remember that some recipe books will abbreviate "tablespoon" with "tbsp" and "teaspoon" will be written as "tsp".

Useful Equivalent Measures:

3 teaspoons = 1 tablespoon

4 tablespoon = 1/4 cup

5 1/3 tablespoons = 1/3 cup

8 tablespoons = 1/2 cup

16 tablespoons = 1 cup

1 tablespoon = 1/2 fluid ounce

1 cup = 8 fluid ounces

1 cup = 1/2 pint

2 cups = 1 pint

4 cups = 1 quart

2 pints = 1 quart

4 quarts = 1 gallon

SOMETHING TO COOK

"Go to the ant, O sluggard, study her ways and learn wisdom;
For though she has no chief, no commander or ruler,
She procures her food in the summer, stores up her provisions in the harvest."

Proverbs 6:6-8

Cooking is Fun!

The recipes in this section are meant to get you started on your culinary journey and to show you what fun cooking can be. All of the recipes listed below can be cooked in your kitchen and many of them work great over an outdoor fire. Recipes with the fire-friendly symbol will include additional instructions for cooking over and in a fire.

Recipe Index

Organizing Your Recipes

As you try out new recipes and discover new favorites, you will want to keep track of those recipes so that you can find them easily when you need them. Below are a few ways in which you might organize your recipe collection:

1. Write them out or tape them onto index cards and file them in a recipe box.

2. Use a small photo album and slip recipes into the clear pockets meant for photos. Larger copies of recipes can simply be folded to fit and the recipe name written on the outside for easy identification.

3. A full sized binder with page protectors is another way to stay organized. Page protectors are clear plastic sheets that allow you to slip an entire page into them. They come with three pre-punched binder holes and are a great way to organize recipes that have been printed off of the computer.

Using one or more of these ideas will make finding that favorite recipe a breeze!

Cornbread

(Makes 8 servings.)

This easy cornbread is delicious served warm with lots of butter!

Ingredients:

1 cup all-purpose flour

1 cup cornmeal

3 tablespoons sugar

1 tablespoon baking powder

1/2 teaspoon salt

2 eggs

1 cup milk (or water)

1/4 cup cooking oil

Directions:

1. Preheat oven to 400° and prepare an 8" x 8" pan (or 9" round pan or cast iron skillet) by coating the inside with a light coat of cooking oil. (Directions for camp fire cooking can be found on page 20.)
2. Mix all of the *dry ingredients* together with a large mixing spoon or wire whisk in a medium sized mixing bowl. In a second bowl, crack open the 2 eggs, milk (or water) and cooking oil. Mix until well blended with wire whisk.
3. Now carefully pour the *wet ingredients* into the bowl containing the dry ingredients and mix until just combined. Do not over mix! There will still be a few lumps and this is ok.
4. Pour the batter into the prepared pan and bake for 25 – 30 minutes, or until a toothpick comes out clean when inserted into the center.
5. Allow the cornbread to cool for about 15 minutes, then cut and serve.

Directions for Cooking Cornbread over a Fire:

The simplest way to bake over a camp fire is with a *camp Dutch oven* (**1**). This piece of equipment is made out of cast iron and has built-in legs for holding it up over hot coals as well as small lip around the top of the lid for helping the coals stay in place.

The only other tools you will need are a 9" round cake pan (**2**), a small metal trivet (**3**) (for holding the cake pan slightly above the surface of the Dutch oven) and a lid lifter (**4**). It is also nice to have a pair of barbecue tongs (**5**). If you do not have the cake pan or trivet, the cornbread can still be cooked over hot coals by simply pouring the batter into the Dutch oven itself.

1. The first step is to preheat your Dutch oven. To do this, prepare a small bed (slightly larger than your camp Dutch oven) of hot, glowing. Place the closed Dutch oven (with the metal trivet sitting on the bottom inside) on top of the coals. Very carefully, using a small shovel (**6**), place more hot, glowing coals on top of the lid. Do not put on so much as to overflow the lid, but just enough to cover it.).

Allow the oven to preheat in this manner while you are mixing up your cornbread batter or for about 10 minutes.

2. When the batter is ready, pour it into the greased 9" round cake pan. Being extremely careful, use the lid lifter to slowly remove the lid and set aside on a clean rock or other clean heat proof surface. Carefully lower the pan of cornbread batter down into the Dutch oven and onto the trivet. Use the tongs to help you do this without burning your fingers. Slowly replace the lid taking care not to knock any ash onto your cornbread. Set a timer for 30 minutes and do not open the lid to peek! Lifting the lid lets valuable heat escape and your cornbread will cook much more slowly.

3. When 30 minutes has passed, remove the Dutch oven from the heat by lifting it by the bail with the lid lifter and placing it on the ground nearby. Next, carefully remove the lid (with the lid lifter) and set it on a clean, fireproof surface such as a rock. Using the tongs (or a table knife), lift one side of the cornbread pan out of the Dutch oven until you can grab it with a hand protected by a hot pad.

4. Allow cornbread to cool for a few minutes, then cut and serve!

This may all sound somewhat complicated the first time you try it, but it is really quite simple! You will find that the camp Dutch oven is a very versatile tool, and if you plan to do much outdoor cooking at all, a worthwhile investment. Make sure to dry all cast iron *very* well after cleaning so it does not rust.

Time Saving Tip:

If you are going to be cooking this recipe while camping, save time by mixing all of the dry ingredients together ahead of time (Bannock is shown here.) and packaging them in a zip top bag. Label the bag with the name of the recipe and a list of the other ingredients to add and you are ready to go!

Pancakes

(Makes 8 servings.)

There is nothing quite like the smell of pancakes floating on the early morning breeze.

Ingredients:

1 cup all-purpose flour

1 cup whole wheat flour

2 tablespoons sugar

2 teaspoons baking powder

1 teaspoon salt

2 eggs

2 cups milk (or water)

2 tablespoons cooking oil

Directions:

1. Preheat a cast iron skillet or griddle over medium – low heat on the stovetop, or on a grill set over red hot coals, while preparing the pancake batter.
2. Mix all of the *dry ingredients* together in a medium sized mixing bowl. In a second bowl, mix the eggs, milk and oil until well blended. A wire whisk works great for this. (To prepare dry ingredients ahead for camping or hiking, see tip on page 29.)
3. Carefully pour the *wet ingredients* into the bowl containing the dry ingredients and mix until just combined. Be careful not to over mix! A few lumps in the batter is ok.
4. Pour a very little oil onto the hot cooking surface and spread with a metal spatula. Using a 1/4 cup measuring cup, drop pancake batter onto the skillet or griddle. Cook for a 3 or 4 minutes (The exact time will vary and will depend on how hot the pan is.) or until the edges of the pancake begin to look dry. Flip and cook on the other side until lightly browned. Enjoy while nice and warm with the topping of your choice.

Bannock

(Makes 8 servings.)

This is the traditional camping bread and is so much fun cooked over a fire!

Ingredients:

4 cups all-purpose flour
3 tablespoons baking powder
1 teaspoon salt

3 tablespoons cooking oil
1 1/2 cups water

Directions:

1. Bannock can easily be cooked on a skillet or griddle like the previous pancake recipe, but it is so very much fun to cook on a stick, this method should be tried at least once. To bake bannock on a stick, locate a few nice clean sticks about 3 – 4 feet long and 1/4 – 1/2 inch in diameter.
2. In a medium sized bowl, mix together the flour, baking powder and salt. (See tip on page 29 for packaging ahead this mixture.)
3. Add the cooking oil and about half of the water. Stir well adding a little more of the water at a time to form a soft dough and then kneed well for about 5 minutes.
4. Form dough into small cakes for frying on a lightly oiled preheated skillet or griddle. For stick cooking, shape a handful of dough into a snake shape about 6 inches long and wrap around the end of the stick.
5. If cooking on a stick, hold over hot coals or low flames and turn slowly. Cook either on a pan or a stick until lightly browned and serve with butter and honey, if desired.

Scrambled Eggs

(Serves 4 average eaters, or 2 really hungry ones.)

Eggs are simple, versatile and great for any meal!

Ingredients:

6 eggs
1/8 teaspoon salt (Just a few dashes.)
dash of pepper
1 tablespoon butter

Directions:

1. Preheat skillet over medium heat on the stovetop, or on a grill set over red hot coals, while preparing the eggs. (This recipe is easy to cut in half if you need to.)
2. Break eggs into a medium sized bowl. Add salt and pepper and beat eggs well with a fork. Drop the tablespoon of butter into the hot skillet to grease it so that the eggs do not stick. Pour in the egg mixture.
3. When the eggs begin to set around the edge, stir gently with a spatula until eggs are thoroughly cooked but before they are dried out. Remove from pan and serve warm.

Hard Boiled Eggs

1. To boil eggs, place them in a small saucepan and cover them with cool water. Bring the water to a boil for 2 minutes, then turn off the heat and place the cover on the pan. After 20 minutes, run cold tap water over the eggs to cool them. Peel and enjoy!

Baked Potato

(Allow one medium sized potato per person.)

A nice hot baked potato is so delicious on a chilly day.

Ingredients:

1 medium sized whole potato for each person (medium sized is about 8-10oz)
salt and pepper
butter, cheese or any favorite topping
aluminum foil

Directions:

1. Begin by scrubbing the potatoes clean.
2. Next, completely wrap each potato in a piece of the heavy duty aluminum foil or in two layers of regular aluminum foil.
3. To bake the potatoes in hot coals, carefully (with a small shovel) bury each potato in the hot coals near the edge of your fire. Make sure the potatoes are completely covered with coals. (Or place in a preheated 350° oven for 60 minutes.)
4. After 40 minutes, use tongs to lift out your potatoes. Allow them to cool slightly for 10 minutes and then carefully wipe off the outside of the foil. Peel back the foil and slice once lengthwise to open. Add salt, pepper, butter or the toppings of your choice.

Roasted Corn

(Allow one ear of corn per person.)

Fresh corn on the cob steamed in its own husk. Yum!

Ingredients:

1 ear of corn per person
1 tablespoon of softened butter for each ear of corn
salt and pepper (if desired)
aluminum foil

Directions:

1. Remove the butter from the refrigerator and allow it to soften by sitting on the counter for about 30 minutes.
2. To prepare the corn, begin by peeling back the husks of the corn but being careful to leave them still attached at the base of the cob. Pull off and throw away the corn silk. Trim off any spots that may have been damaged by worms or other insects and rinse the cobs well. Pat with a clean towel to dry.
3. Next, spread about 1 tablespoon of butter all over each ear. Lightly salt and pepper each one and carefully fold the corn husks back up and over the ears of corn.
4. Next, completely wrap each ear of corn in a piece of the heavy duty aluminum foil or in two layers of regular aluminum foil.
5. To cook the corn, place on a grill positioned above a hot bed of coals. Roast for 35 minutes turning half way through. (Or place in a preheated 375° oven for 30 minutes.) When done (the kernels will be tender), peel back the husks and enjoy!

Granola

(Makes about 6 servings.)

This simple granola makes a great trail snack to take on hikes.

Ingredients:

5 cups rolled oats
1/4 cup flour
1/3 cup oil
1/2 cup maple syrup or honey
1/4 cup brown sugar

1 teaspoon cinnamon
1/4 teaspoon salt
1/2 cup raisins

Directions:

1. Preheat oven to 375°.
2. In a large bowl, combine the oats and flour. Mix well and set aside.
3. In a small saucepan on the stovetop, mix together the oil, maple syrup or honey, brown sugar, cinnamon and salt. Heat this mixture, while stirring often, until the brown sugar dissolves.
4. When the sugar has dissolved, remove the pan from the heat and carefully pour over the oats and flour mixture, while stirring, until the two mixtures are combined well.
5. Spread the uncooked granola on a cookie sheet and bake for 10 minutes.
6. After 10 minutes, pull the cookie sheet out of the oven and gently stir the granola so that the edges do not get too dark. After stirring, carefully return the granola to the oven and bake for 5 minutes longer.
7. After the additional 5 minutes, remove the cookie sheet and allow granola to cool completely. Once it is cool, mix in the raisins and store in a glass jar or other airtight container.

Chocolaty Brownies

(Makes about 15 large brownies.)

These yummy brownies are made extra chocolaty with the addition of chocolate chips. They make the perfect treat to celebrate that special feast day!

Ingredients:

1 cup oil

2 cups sugar

2 teaspoons vanilla

4 eggs

3/4 cup cocoa

1 cup all purpose flour

1/2 teaspoon baking powder

1/2 teaspoon salt

1 cup chocolate chips
  (milk chocolate or semi sweet)

Directions:

1. Preheat oven to 350° and prepare a 9" x 13" pan by coating it with a light coat of cooking oil.
2. In a large mixing bowl combine oil, sugar and vanilla and mix well with a spoon or large whisk.
3. Add the eggs next and stir well so that they are completely blended.
4. Next, stir in the cocoa. After the cocoa has been mixed in completely, add the flour, baking powder and salt and stir until all of the ingredients are combined.
5. Add in the cup of chocolate chips and stir.
6. Pour the batter into the prepared pan and bake for 35 minutes.
7. When the brownies are done, allow the pan to cool before cutting.

Hot Chocolate Mix

(Makes 4 servings.)

This delicious, homemade hot chocolate mix is perfect for
enjoying around the campfire, or giving as a gift.

Ingredients:

1 1/3 cups powdered milk

1/8 cup cocoa

1/3 cup tablespoons sugar

Directions:

1. Combine all of the ingredients together in a
   small bowl and mix well.
2. Store in an airtight container such as a glass jar.
3. To make a cup of hot chocolate, scoop out 1/2 cup
   of the mix and place it into a 12 ounce mug. Fill
   the mug with hot water (which can be heated in
   a kettle on a grill over your campfire) and stir
   well.
4. Add marshmallows if you like them and enjoy!

Time Saving Tip:

If you are planning to have a
cup of this hot chocolate while
camping or on a hike, save
time and backpack space by
mixing all of the ingredients
together ahead of time and
packaging them in a snack
sized zip top bag. This bag can
be stuffed inside your cup
inside your pack or mess kit.

My Cooking Notes & Ideas:

_____

_____

_____

_____

_____

_____

_____

_____

_____

_____

_____

A Recipe Card:

If you would like to share these (or any other) recipes with a friend,
simply make copies of the recipe card below.
Print them onto cardstock and cut out.

A Recipe For:

The Tin Cup

Tin is a fairly soft metal that has been mined since 3,000 BC and is even mentioned a few times in the Bible (See Numbers 31:22 and Ezekiel 27:12.). The first tin shop in Colonial America opened in 1740 and one year later the first tin peddler set out in his cart to sell his tin cups, pie pans, milk pails, pots and more to the people of New England.

Antique Handmade Tin Cup

Vintage Enamelware Cups

The tin smith would spend the snowy winter months in his shop making all sorts of useful things with tin. When the weather began to warm he would set out with his horse and cart. Tin items were an important part of every household, and because it was an inexpensive metal, it was sometimes called the "poor man's silver".

During the time of the Westward Expansion we think of the pioneers with their tin pails and tubs strapped to their covered wagons and the men of the California Gold Rush panning for gold with their tin pans. Every one room school house had a water pail with a tin dipper for the children to drink from and every adventurer and explorer had their tin cup strapped to the outside of their pack so that it would be handy for dipping out a cool drink from a stream.

These days, it is not safe to drink from creeks and streams without first filtering the water, but a "tin cup" is still an essential part of every

Collapsible Aluminum Cups

Stainless Camper's Cup with Folding Handle

camper, backpacker and hiker's gear. Today's "tin cups" however, are rarely made of tin. Instead they are stainless steel, enamelware and titanium. They come in dozens of different shapes and sizes, are great for water, hot chocolate, soup, (Be careful if the cup is hot!) and more. They are quite a useful addition to your haversack (see page 69), satchel or backpack, especially when paired with a small mess kit.

What is a Mess Kit?

A mess kit is a small, lightweight set of eating or cooking tools used by soldiers as well as campers and backpackers. The word "mess" is a very old term (dating back to at least the 13th century) for a portion of food. The items in a mess kit usually nest together with folding handles to make the kit as compact as possible. Some parts of the kit can be used for more than one purpose, such as plates being used as lids or skillets.

World War II Mess Kit
(1944)

Camping Mess Kit

St. Dominic Savio

St. Dominic Savio was born on April 2, 1842 near Turin, Italy (This is the same region in which St. John Bosco lived. See page 12.) and was one of ten siblings. His parents were diligent in teaching him about his Faith, and from a very early age Dominic was often found praying by himself when at work and at play. He was a cheerful and fun-loving boy who had many friends and after receiving his First Communion, Dominic had an even greater desire to please Jesus and to live a holy life.

In 1854, at the age of 12, Dominic was sent to St. John Bosco's school, the Oratory of St Francis de Sales to study to become a priest. Dominic was *overjoyed* to be able to go to the Oratory and learn from Father Bosco. He soon became a leader among the boys at the school and gathered together a group to become the Company of the Immaculate Conception. This group took it upon themselves to clean and care for the school as well as to befriend the boys of the school who were often left out.

When he was 14 years old, Dominic became ill and was sent back to his home to recover. He quickly grew worse, however, and on March 9, 1857, less than a month before he turned 15, Dominic went to Heaven to be with Our Lord forever.
St. Dominic Savio, patron saint of boys, pray for us!

"I am not capable of doing big things, but I want to do everything, even the smallest things, for the greater glory of God."

~ St Dominic Savio

A STITCH IN TIME

"Do not grow slack but be fervent in spirit; He whom you serve is the Lord. Rejoice in hope, be patient under trial, persevere in prayer."

Romans 12:11-12

Do Boys Sew?

Yes! In fact, *many* men sew and have done so for all of history. Explorers, adventurers and the military men of nearly every nation all carry with them some sort of sewing kit to make necessary repairs to their clothing and gear.

The interesting little kit to the left is one type of vintage military pocket sewing kit. It is made up of a metal tube with a lid. To save space inside, the *thimble* fits into a hole in the lid, while the slender, brass needle holder would have been slipped into the hole in the center of a small spool of thread. This one is most likely from the US military but the German soldiers carried a very similar kit.

This next one (on the left) is a World War II era Canadian soldier's sewing kit with a date stamp of 1942. It is made up of a series of three pockets which contain sewing thread, sock darning yarn, patches, pins, needles and extra uniform buttons. These sewing kits were folded up from the bottom and tied to keep the supplies from falling out.

This last example (to the right) is a vintage, official Boy Scouts of America sewing kit. This little kit would have contained a small pair of scissors, pins, needles, a card of different threads and a small assortment of buttons. A boy would have been well prepared indeed with a kit like this in his pack.

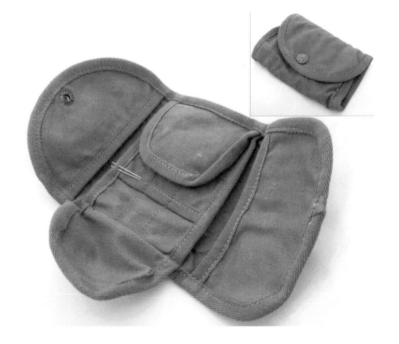

Sew Simple

All the supplies you really need to begin some simple sewing are a needle or two, a few straight pins, a spool of thread and a pair of scissors (Your pocket knife could easily replace the scissors if you needed it to.). On page 61 you will find instructions for making your own compact sewing kit, but first here are some simple directions for getting started.

1. First, cut a piece of thread about 18 inches long and thread your needle.

2. Pull one end of the thread so that it is slightly longer than the other. Tie a single knot in this end. Make sure you are only catching one thread in the knot. The trick to sewing with a single thread is to hold both the thread *and* the needle when pulling a stitch tight. This way your needle does not come unthreaded.

3. Because this is just practice, find a scrap piece of fabric to make a few stitches on. Old outgrown clothing that is headed for the rag box is the perfect thing. Start by coming up through the underside of the fabric and pull gently until the knot stops the thread. Do not yank hard on the thread or your knot might pop right through the fabric!

4. The next step is to secure the thread in the fabric so that it does not pull out accidently. Begin by pushing the needle back into the fabric slightly behind where it just came out (Step 1), about 1/8 inch away or less, and then pushing it back up again slightly past the spot where the needle first came through (Step 2). This is called a *backstitch*, and it helps to anchor the thread in the fabric.

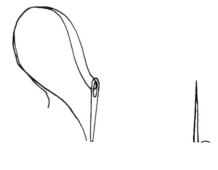

Step 1   Step 2

5. Now you are ready to begin a basic running stitch. Simply push the needle in and out of the fabric trying to make your stitches no more than 1/4" long. Be careful not to pull your thread out of your needle and do not pull too hard on the thread. Pulling too hard will make your stitches gather and the fabric pucker. Keep the stitching smooth and flat as you go, but stop before your thread runs out.

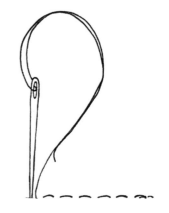

Running Stitch

6. You will need a 3 or 4 inch tail of thread for securing it at the end of the line of stitching, so do not stitch all the way to the end of your thread. The simplest way to secure it is to make 2 or 3 tiny backstitches and then a couple of simple knots. Now snip the thread 1/4 inch from the fabric and place your needle back into your sewing kit or pincushion. That's it!

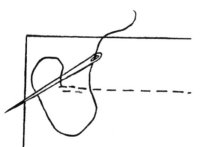

A Simple Knot

One more stitch that will be helpful in constructing your sewing kit is the *blanket stitch*. It is called the blanket stitch because it was originally used to reinforce the edges of thick, wool blankets. It works great when sewing together and trimming the edges of fabric that will not fray, such as felt. The blanket stitch shown on the sewing kit is done with two lengths of thread used together at the same time for added thickness.

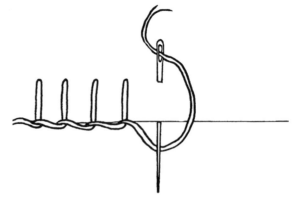

Blanket Stitch

SOMETHING TO SEW

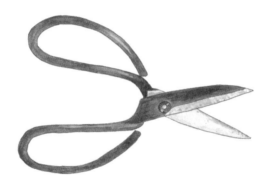

"Whenever you begin any good work you should first of all make a most
pressing appeal to Christ our Lord to bring it to perfection."

~ St. Benedict of Nursia

A Sewing Kit

This simple and compact emergency sewing kit is a great way to safely carry with you all that you would need for any small repair.

> **Supplies Needed:**
>
> - A small scrap of felt 7" x 2 1/2" (Felt made up of some, or all wool will hold up better under frequent use.)
> - Sewing thread, needle and pins
> - A match holder (From the camping section of your local discount or sporting goods store.)
> - Various supplies for contents such as safety pins, buttons, scraps of fabric for patches, thread and needles.

1. Using a ruler and a pencil, mark a 7" x 2 1/2" rectangle on your piece of felt. Cut out this rectangle.

2. Fold up 1 3/4" on one end and pin in place. This will be the pocket in your kit.

3. Thread a needle with about 3 feet of thread, double it over and knot the two ends together. You will be stitching with two threads at once.

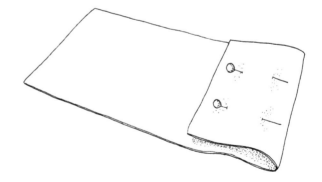

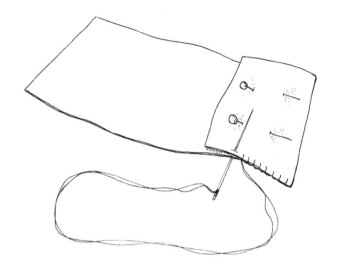

4. Beginning at the crease of the fold on one side, insert your needle and pull the thread until the knot meets the felt to stop your thread from pulling all of the way through.

5. To sew up the two sides of the pocket any stitch will work, but a blanket stitch (as show on page 58) looks very nice and is a great stitch for sewing felt.

6. When you come to the end of the first side of the pocket, secure the thread (see page 58) and clip the thread. Tie another knot at the end of the thread and stitch up the second side of the pocket.

7. Your sewing kit is now finished! All that remains is to fill it with the items you will need.

For storing a bit of thread, snip a small piece of lightweight cardboard (such as from a cereal box or other packaging) about 1 1/2" x 1/2". Cut 2 or 3 tiny slits into the side of the cardboard and wrap a couple of yards of 2 or 3 different color threads around it, securing the ends of the thread in the slits so that it does not unwind.

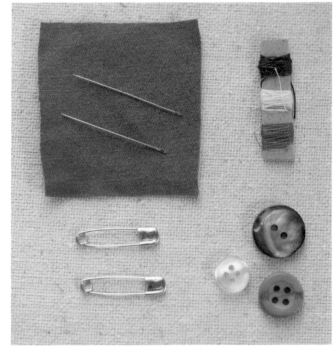

When filled, roll the felt kit from the bottom up and insert it into the match holder. The hard plastic of the holder keeps the needles from poking through and keeps everything nice and dry. Don't worry about needing scissors in your kit, as you can use your pocket knife to snip the thread, or simply break it. You are now ready to stitch anywhere!

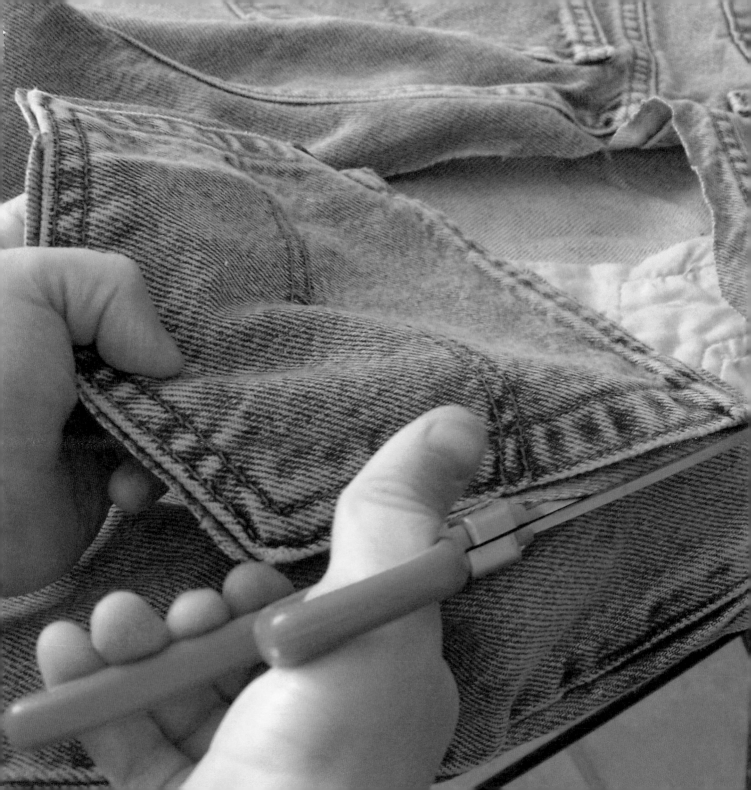

A Pot Holder

One of the best sources for supplies for your projects is old items of clothing that are torn or stained beyond use. These easy and useful pot holders are made from the back pockets of men's jeans!

Supplies Needed:

- An old pair of men's blue jeans or other pants
- An old flannel shirt, worn out T-shirt or old towel for insulation
- Sewing thread, needle and pins

---

1. Using a pair of scissors carefully cut a back pocket out of the back of the jeans. Make sure to leave the fabric that the pocket is sewn onto, attached to the pocket.

2. Once you have freed the pocket from the jeans, you are ready to cut a layer (or more) of some sort of insulation. This is important as it will help to protect your hands from the hot pot or pan handles. You can use almost any type of natural fiber fabric (such as cotton or wool) but old worn out towels, flannel (a type of soft, cotton fabric) shirts or T-shirts work especially well. If you are using a thicker fabric such as toweling, one layer will work fine. If you are using a thinner fabric such as flannel or T-shirt fabric, using 2 or 3 layers will provide more protection.

Don't Forget:

If you are cutting up an old shirt for the insulation part of these pot holders, don't forget to snip off any buttons to save for future projects or to keep in your sewing kit.

3. To cut out the insulation, pin the pocket to the fabric and cut around it being careful not to cut into the pocket.

After it has been cut out, trim off about 3/8" from the sides and bottom of the insulation. This is so that it will fit inside the pocket.

4. Now insert the insulation into the pocket making sure it is smooth and not folded or wrinkled. Thread one of your needles with matching thread. If you need a bit of help with the sewing, refer to the instructions on pages 57 and 58. After a couple of backstitches to anchor the thread, sew across the open top of the pocket using a running stitch. This is to keep the insulation in the pocket.

5. It is a good idea to place two *tacking stitches* in your pot holder to keep the insulation fabric in place and prevent it from bunching up when the pot holder is washed. A tacking stitch is made by simply going in and out of the fabric (through all layers), 2 or 3 times and then tying off. It is very much like sewing on a button (See page 76.), but without the button.

The illustration to the right shows the best areas to place the tacking stitches.

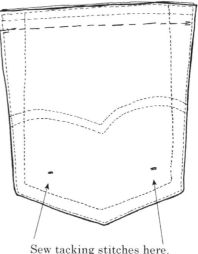

Sew tacking stitches here.

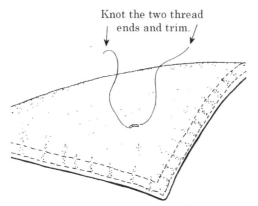

Knot the two thread ends and trim.

6. Begin and end the tacking stitches on the same side of the pot holder leaving about 3 inches of thread on each end. Make a square knot (See page 81.) with the two ends and then trim to 1/4 inch to finish off.

That is it! Your pot holder is now complete and ready for action in the kitchen or by the fire. These are an easy way to make use of old worn out clothing and also make great gifts.

A Haversack

The haversack is a simple, all purpose bag that has been used by both military men and civilians since the early 1800's. It is made with a single strap, worn either over the shoulder or across the chest, and can hold anything needed for a short hike, a day trip or backyard adventure!

> **Supplies Needed:**
>
> - An old pair of men's pants. The bigger and baggier the better. A great place to find the perfect pair is your local thrift store or resale shop.
> - Two buttons harvested from the pants or from your stash of saved buttons.
> - Sewing thread, needle, pins and clothes iron.

1. First, lay out the pair of pants on the floor making everything as smooth as possible.

   Starting from the bottom of one of the pants legs, measure up the leg and mark it at 22 inches all the way across the leg.

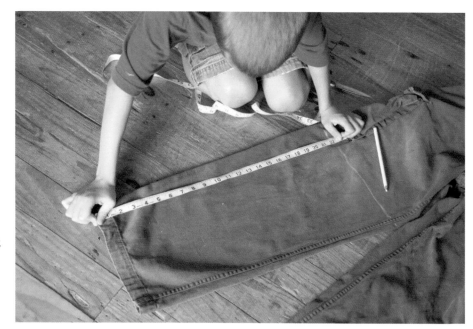

A regular pencil works fine for marking light colored fabrics, and a white color pencil is great for darker ones.

2. Cut across the line you have made to separate the lower part that will become your haversack from the rest of the pants. Set this part aside for now.

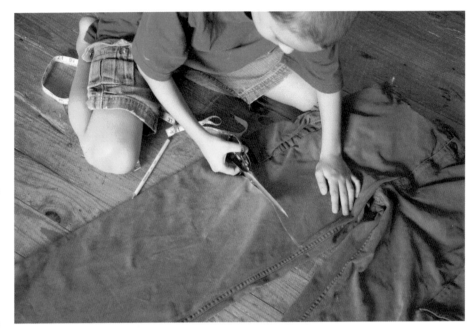

3. On the second pant leg draw two line 3 1/2 inches apart from the bottom cuff all the way up to the waistband. A yardstick will make this job easier. This 3 1/2 inch wide strip will become your shoulder strap. Cut it as long as possible now and you will be able to shorten it later.

4. Taking the 3 1/2 wide strip, rip out the stitching (using a *seam ripper* or a pair of scissors) in the cuff area to make it as long as possible.

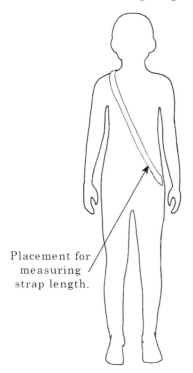

Placement for measuring strap length.

5. Very carefully, press the strap, flat with a hot iron. After getting it smooth, use your fingers to turn the long edges of the strap inward about 1/4" while pressing with the iron. Be careful not to burn your fingers! Once the edges have been pressed well, fold the entire strap in half lengthwise and press once more.

Now at this point, we need to measure the strap to get it the correct length. Place the strap over one shoulder and bring it across your chest to your hip bone. This is probably where you will want the top of your haversack to be when you are wearing it. If you would rather it longer or shorter, feel free to adjust the placement. This is your sack so it should be just how you like it. Cut the strap ends so that they land about where you want the top of the haversack to be.

6. Place a few pins in the folded and pressed strap to hold it in place and thread a needle to begin stitching the edges together. The thread in the picture is red so that it shows up well. Choosing a color that matches your fabric will make the finished strap look neater. Stitch along the entire edge, press and set aside.

7. Taking the 22 inch long section of pant leg that you cut off, turn it inside out and line up the cut edge neatly. Pin the two layers together as shown in the photo.

8. Beginning at one end of the pant leg, stitch across using small stitches about 1/2 inch from the cut edge. Red thread has been used here so that it shows up well, but a matching color is recommended.

After stitching across once, it is a good idea to go back and sew a

second line of stitching just under the first. This reinforces the bottom of your haversack and creates a good strong seam.

When you have knotted and trimmed the thread, turn the bag right side out and press well with a hot iron.

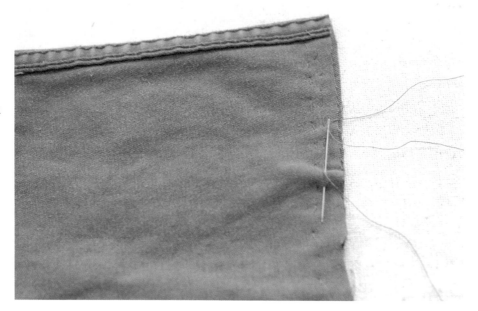

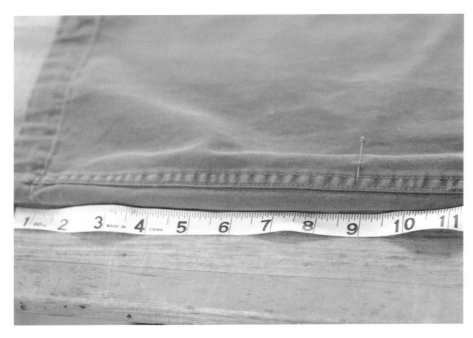

9. To find the correct spot to sew the strap onto the bag, measure 9 inches from the top of the bag (Which is actually the cuff of the pant leg.) and mark this point with a pin or a small pencil mark.

10. Position one end of the strap over the side seam of the bag with the 9 inch marker in the *center* of the end of the strap. Make sure the strap end overlaps the seam about 1/4 of an inch.

Repeat strap placement and pinning on the other side of the haversack being careful there is no twist in the strap. Make sure you are only pinning through one layer of the bag when attaching the strap ends. You do not want to pin the front of the bag to the back of it.

11. Using 2 strands of thread, stitch the strap ends to the side seams of the bag. Reinforce by stitching a second time across.

Do not worry about the slight fraying on the ends of the strap. This will not cause a problem and adds a bit of a rugged look to the finished sack.

12. For the final step, sew on a button over the stitching that secures the strap end to the bag. This step is optional, but it is a neat touch and it gives the impression that the strap is buttoned to the bag.

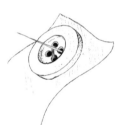

If you are adding on a button, do not cut the thread after attaching the strap to the bag. Instead, put the needle through one of the holes in a button and slide the button down until it rests in the correct spot. While holding the button in place, push the needle down through the hole opposite the one it just came up through. Repeat these steps until you have made 3 or 4 stitches across the button. If you are using a button with only two holes, you are done. If you have a 4-hole button, repeat with the remaining 2 holes. When you are finished stitching, bring the thread to the inside of the bag, knot it and cut the thread.

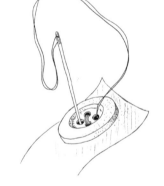

Congratulations! You have created a terrific and useful haversack to take with you anywhere. For ideas on what to pack for your adventures, take a peek at the next chapter.

[76]

WHAT'S IN YOUR SACK?

"Start by doing what is necessary, then do what is possible, and
suddenly you are doing the impossible."

~ St. Francis of Assisi

Haversack Content Ideas

These are only a few suggestions as to what to put into your haversack. The possibilities are as endless as your imagination!

The Items Shown in the Photo to the Left:

1. Assorted Field Guides
2. Snacks
3. Bandana
4. Water Bottle or Canteen
5. Pocket Knife
6. Sewing Kit
7. Length of Lightweight Rope
8. "Tin" Cup
9. Tenner or Pocket Shrine
10. Tinder Box
11. First Aid Kit
12. Notebook & Pencil
13. Eating Utensils

1. **Assorted Field Guides:** A couple of your favorite field guides are great to have along to help in identifying local birds, insects etc.

2. **Snacks:** The granola recipe on page 41 makes a nice energy-boosting treat, but any healthy snack such as dried fruit or crackers will work.

3. **Bandana:** The simple bandana is one of the most versatile and useful things that you can carry with you. It is a great mini picnic cloth when spread out on the ground to make a clean area to lay your snacks. It can be a bandage, handkerchief or napkin or small treasures can be tied in the center of your bandana so that they do not get lost in your haversack.

4. **Water Bottle or Canteen:** This is probably one of the most important things to have with you if you are going to be outdoors for any length of time. Not only for drinking, but a little water on a clean bandana is great for cooling a hot face or wiping dirty hands.

5. **Pocket Knife:** Owning a pocket knife is a big step in a boy's life. If your parents have allowed you to have a pocket knife of your own, it means that they believe you are responsible enough to be trusted with the keeping of something that could be quite dangerous if not used with care. Chances are, either your friends or older siblings also have pocket knives of their own. Many knives look similar and when out camping or hiking it is possible to get your knife confused with someone else's. If your knife has a ring on one end of it you can easily mark your knife by attaching a medal of your favorite saint to it. (The medal in the photo is of Blessed Francis Seelos.) See the Further Reading section for a great book on whittling on page 106.

6. **Sewing Kit:** Don't forget to take your emergency sewing kit along. If you haven't made one yet, turn to page 61 to see how easy it is to carry everything you need to repair a small rip or replace a button.

7. **Length of Lightweight Rope:** Carrying a bit (2 to 3 yards) of rope can come in very handy indeed. To keep the ends from unraveling, wrap them in a small piece of duct tape. If you find yourself with nothing to tie up, use it to practice your knot tying skills. You can see the Further Reading section on page 106 for knot tying book suggestions but you can begin by learning the very useful square knot right here:

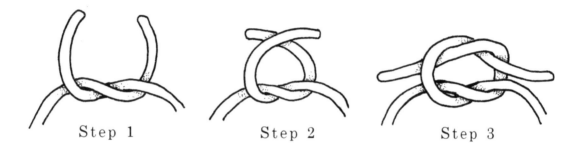

Step 1   Step 2   Step 3

8. **"Tin" Cup:** The type of cup pictured here and on page 78 is called a "Sierra cup". The wide opening on these cups makes them great for both drinking out of and using as a bowl for eating. Because they are stainless steel, they also work as a small pot for cooking or warming up food or beverage. The really neat thing about this particular style of cup is that the handle folds down for packing! (For more about tin cups, see page 49.)

9. **Tenner or Pocket Shrine:** Carry your Faith with you always! Now this does not necessarily mean carrying it in your hands, but rather in your heart and mind. However, if you would like to have something with you to remind you to pray and help you to stay on the right track, you might consider a tenner or pocket shrine.

Tenners are simple single decade rosaries that began to be used by *men* hundreds of years ago because they were small and could be easily carried in their pockets. They consist of a crucifix, an Our Father bead, ten Hail Mary's and a medal. (The term tenner comes from the ten Hail Mary beads used.) The medal can be anything that has meaning to the owner such as a patron saint or even a scapular or miraculous medal. You could make a tenner yourself, or use any other type of single decade rosary.

Pocket shrines are very small capsules containing a tiny, 1-inch high figure of Jesus, Mary or a saint. The little statues were made in brass, silver, pewter or lead and were carried in the pockets of soldiers, salesmen and other men who traveled away from home for their living. They were used to help them to keep focused on God when times got tough. The St. Joseph statue on the left is from WWII era while the little figure of Our Lady on the right is probably from WWI or earlier. Even though these can still be found fairly easily, any small statue would work as well.

10. **Tinder Box:** This little piece of your equipment can make lighting that campfire much easier. If you have not yet made your own tinderbox, see pages 19 -20 for ideas.

11. **First Aid Kit:** Where first aid kits are concerned, it doesn't have to be very big to be a big help. Even something as small as a blister on your foot can really take the fun out of a hike or walk. Having a few bandaids with you is always a good idea but a more complete kit can be made out of an old candy tin:

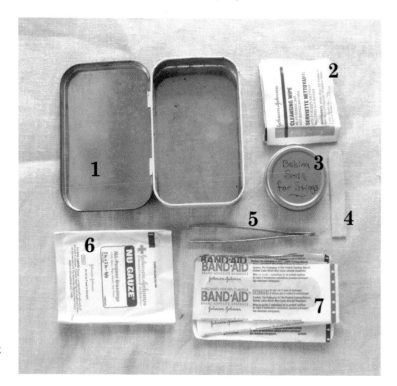

1. *Empty Candy Tin*
2. *Alcohol Wipes* (From another larger first aid kit.)
3. *Two Teaspoons of Baking Soda* (Mixing baking soda with enough water to make a paste will quickly relieve the pain and swelling of many insect stings. You would only need to add about 1/2 teaspoon of water for 2 teaspoons of baking soda.)

4. *A Half of a Wooden Popsicle Stick* (For stirring the baking soda after the water has been added.)
5. *Tweezers* (For splinter removal.)
6. *Gauze* (To cover a larger wound. Use the bandaids as tape to hold in place.)
7. *Assorted Bandaids* (Included here are regular, knuckle and butterfly bandaids.)

[83]

12. **Notebook and Pencil:** Having something to write on and write with stashed in your haversack is a great idea. A small lightweight notebook works great for making nature observations such as bird, insect or animal sightings and quick sketches of interesting plants and leaf rubbings (See page 87 for ideas on outfitting a *naturalist's* haversack.). You can use it to leave notes for friends or family, write a letter or a list and make a paper airplane.

13. **Eating Utensils:** Of course you always have with you some of the best eating utensils, your very own fingers, but sometimes it is nice to be prepared for a picnic with something a bit more civilized. The two sets pictured here are very compact and convenient, but just tossing a simple spoon into your bag will go a long way when you need to stir a cup of hot chocolate or sip on soup.

These are just a few ideas to get you started in outfitting your own haversack. Keep in mind that the different items you pack might change depending on the plans you have, such as taking along a compass and emergency whistle for a long hike. The important thing is to prepare for your possible needs and wants *before* they occur and to have fun! You can use the space on the facing page to keep a running list of any other items you would like to add to your list.

Other Things to Put
in My Haversack:

The Naturalist's Sack

A *naturalist* is someone who observes the plants and creatures around him. He becomes familiar with the natural world and studies God's wondrous creation in order to better appreciate and learn all he can about it. Whether in a field, the woods, the shore or your own backyard, there are amazing things to see if you will look closely.

Below are a few ideas for what you might like to include in your naturalist's haversack:

- A field guide or two
- Nature notebook and pencil (See page 89)
- Binoculars
- Magnifying glass
- Pocket microscope
- Portable plant press (see page 95)
- Tweezers
- Small containers
- Small zip-top bags
- Pocket knife
- A bandana

Drawing or simply listing the different species of plants and animals that you see is a great way to keep a record of what you have come across in your explorations. Naturalists call this a *life list* because they continue to add to it throughout their life. It is a record of the species that you have positively identified in your observations. Some keep life lists only for birds and some only for insects or reptiles. Your list can be anything (or everything) you like. Your notebook needs only to be lightweight and fit into your haversack or *field bag*. In the next section you will find instructions for making a simple nature notebook of your own so that you can begin your own life list or simply have fun sketching the world around you.

A Nature Notebook

Sketching the creatures and plants that you observe is a great way to learn even more about them. The simple little book shown here is just right for recording your finds and even has pockets to tuck a favorite leaf or feather into.

Supplies Needed:

- One sheet of 8 1/2" x 11"cardstock (any color you like)
- 4 Sheets of 8 1/2" x 11" plain paper (24lb paper is best, but any will do)
- A medium sized needle and waxed dental floss
- 4 clothes pins, a thumb tack and craft glue
- The optional labels on page 100

1. Measure and cut off 2 inches from one of the 8 1/2 inch ends of the cardstock. (See illustration to the right.)

   Do not simply throw away this scrap, as it makes a great book mark!

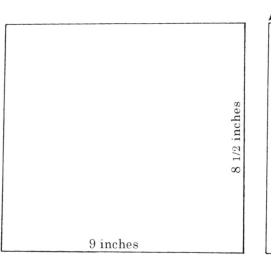

2 inches

8 1/2 inches

9 inches

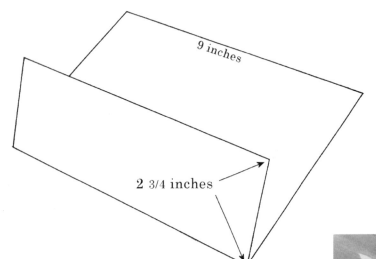

9 inches

2 3/4 inches

2. Along one of the 9 inch sides, fold up a section of the cardstock 2 3/4 inches wide.

An easy way to do this is to measure and mark two dots at the 2 3/4 inch point on either end and then lay the ruler across the cardstock to connect the dots.

Lift up the cardstock and fold against the ruler for a nice neat crease. Remove the ruler and complete the fold. This folded area will become two pockets in the cover of your book.

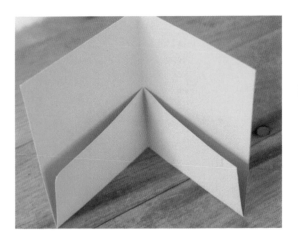

3. Now fold the cardstock in half being, careful to match up the corners, and crease well. This is your book cover. Set it aside for now and let's make the pages.

4. Measure halfway across the 11 inch long side of the papers and cut in them in half. This will give you 4 sheets of paper creating 8 - 81/2 x 51/2 inch sheets. Taking 4 of the smaller sheets stacked together, fold in half once again taking care to match up the corners and crease well.

Repeat with the remaining 4 sheets and then place all 8 sheets stacked together.

5. Center the stack of pages on top of the cover and place a clothespin on each side to hold everything in place. Using the tack, punch holes about 1/2 inch apart down the center crease of the book. Make sure to push the tack through all of the layers. These will be the holes for the needle to go through. It does not matter how many holes that you end up with, the very important thing,

however, is that there are an *odd number* of holes (Usually there are about 9.). Having an odd number of holes is necessary so that the stitching in the next step comes out correctly. Make sure to protect your work surface from holes when using the tack. A cutting board or an old phone book both work well.

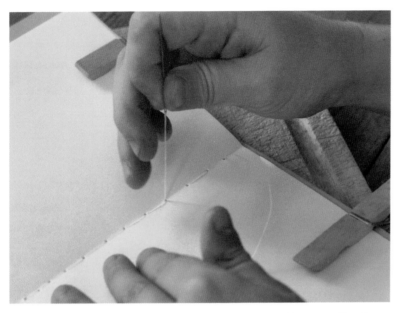

6. Thread your needle with about 2 1/2 feet of waxed dental floss. The floss is used for sewing the spine of your book because it is so much stronger than thread. Starting on the inside of the book, begin by putting the needle into the first hole at one end of the center crease. *Leave a 3 inch tail of the floss on the inside of the book for tying off when you are finished sewing.* This is very important!

Now begin the stitching by putting the needle down into the very next hole and pulling the floss back into the center of the book. Continue going in and out of the holes until you come to the last hole. After reaching the last hole at the end of the book, simply put the needle into the closest hole again and begin to work your way back up the spine going in and out of the holes the same way.

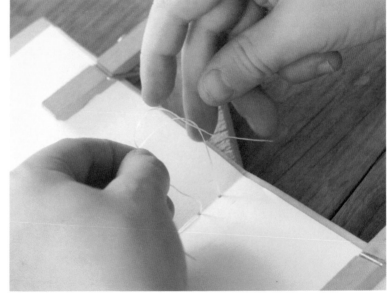

7. After pulling the thread into the center of the book in the *second* to last hole, trim the floss leaving another 3 inch tail. Tie the two ends together using a square knot or any other favorite knot. Trim remaining tails to 1/4 inch.

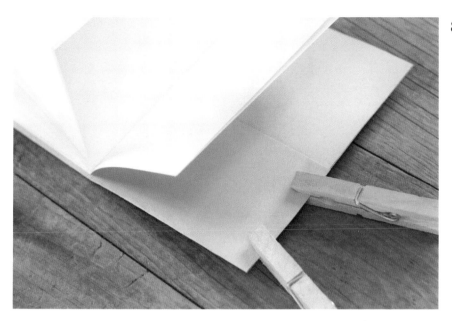

8. Now your book is nearly complete. To finish off the two pockets, place a thin bead of glue between the pocket and the book cover and hold in place with the clothes pins until dry. If your book does not lie flat when closed, it may be necessary at this point to press it under another larger book (such as a dictionary) for a few hours or overnight.

9. The final step is to put a title on your new nature notebook. This can be one of your own design, or you can make a copy of the ones provided on page 100.

   Now get outside and start filling it up with your amazing findings!

A Portable Plant Press

Collecting leaves and flowers for pressing is easy with this small, portable plant press. The press keeps them from being crushed in your sack before getting them home.

> **Supplies Needed:**
>
> - 1 baby's board book (The thrift store or second-hand shop is a great place to find these.)
> - 1 or 2 Sheets of cardstock (Depending on the size of your book.)
> - Duct tape
> - Medium grit sandpaper and craft glue
> - 1 large rubber band

1. When choosing a board book for this project, look for one 5 or 6 inches tall without any pop-ups, flaps or extras on the inside.

   Begin by using a piece of medium grit sandpaper and sanding all over the covers and spine to rough up the surface slightly. This will make the glue stick well so that your new cover will not peel off. Do not sand too much, just enough to remove the shine on the book's surface.

1/4 inch from edge

2. Lay the board book on the corner of a sheet of cardstock with the spine of the book extending 1/4 inch past the edge of the cardstock.

3. Carefully trace around the book and cut out the cardstock. Repeat on the same sheet of cardstock if there is room, or on a separate sheet if you need to.

4. You now have two new covers for your plant press. Lay the covers onto the board book to check the size. Trim the cardstock if any part of it overhangs the book covers.

5. Before gluing, protect your work surface with newspaper or other scrap paper.

Apply craft glue to one of the cardstock covers and spread until all of the area is covered. Place onto book lining up the edges and corners carefully and pressing with fingers till smooth. Repeat with the second cover.

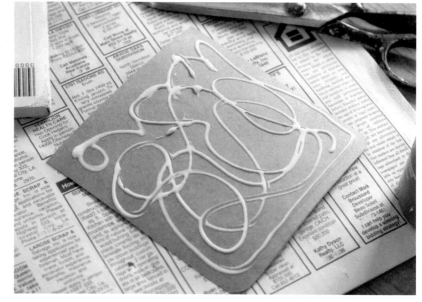

[97]

6. Cut a piece of duct tape slightly longer than the spine of your book. Lay the duct tape sticky side up on your work surface and place the book spine carefully over about 1/3 of the width of the tape.

After the book is placed correctly onto the tape, wrap the duct tape around the spine and trim off the extra on each end. Press and smooth the tape well.

7. If you would like to use one of the labels on page 101 or 102, make a copy of it, cut it out along the gray dotted lines and glue it into place.

Your Portable Plant Press is now ready for action! Simply insert specimens between the pages and place the rubber band around the book to keep it closed. You can allow them to dry there, or transfer them to a larger press after returning home.

"How many are your works, oh Lord!
In wisdom you have made them all,
the earth is full of your creatures."

Psalm 104:24

NATURE NOTEBOOK LABELS

To use these labels on your Nature Notebooks, simply make a copy of them,
clip along the gray dotted lines and glue into place,

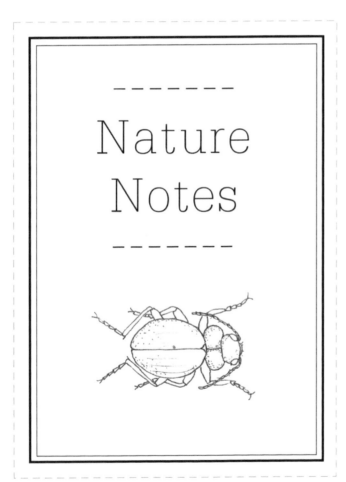

PLANT PRESS LABELS

To use these labels on your Portable Plant Press, simply make a copy of them, clip along the gray dotted lines and glue into place. Choose the size that best fits the board book you are using.

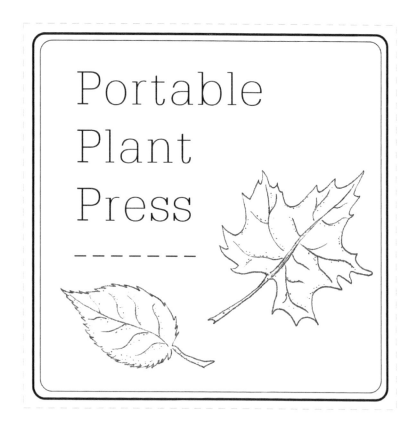

This is a 4 inch label for Portable Plant Presses 5 inches and smaller.

Portable Plant Press

- - - - - - - -

This is a 4 inch label for Portable Plant Presses 6 inches or larger.

"Do good everywhere, so that everyone
can say: This is a son of Christ."

~ St. Pio of Pietrelcina

GLOSSARY

Backstitch – A backstitch is used to anchor a thread when beginning or ending a line of stitching. (See page 57.)

Blanket Stitch – A sewing stitch originally used to reinforce the edges of thick, wool blankets. (See page 58.)

Camp Dutch Oven – A large cast iron pot made with short legs to allow it to sit above hot coals, and a lid with a lip or flange around the edge so that coals can be piled on top allowing the heat to come from above and below at the same time.

Coals –The hot, glowing or smoldering fragments of wood or coal left from a fire.

Cooking Tripod – A set of three iron rods (each about 3 feet in length) attached at the top to make a "tepee" which is positioned over a fire. A chain is suspended from the point where the poles come together and a pot or kettle is hung from the chain over the fire using a hook.

Dry Ingredients – The ingredients in a recipe which are not wet or damp. Examples include flour, sugar, baking powder, spices and salt.

Embers – Coals that have cooled down enough so that they have stopped glowing.

Field Bag – The term used for any bag or sack used to carry the tools of a naturalist.

Firestarters – This term usually refers to some type of man-made tinder. (See page 18-20.)

Kindling – Material for starting a fire, such as small sticks of dry wood used to help build the fire after the tinder is lit.

Life List – A lifelong record kept of the species you have identified in your nature observations.

Naturalist – Someone who studies the natural world around him.

Tacking Stitch – A tacking stitch is made by simply going in and out of the fabric (through all layers), 2 or 3 times and then tying off. (See page 67.)

Tenner – A simple single decade rosaries that began to be used by men hundreds of years ago because they were small and could be easily carried in their pockets. (See page 82.)

Thimble – A small metal cup made to fit over a finger while sewing to protect it from being pierced by the needle.

Tinder – Any dry, easily flammable material used for getting a fire started and lighting the kindling.

Seam Ripper – A handy tool for breaking and removing stitches from seams or any other place you may not want them. Look for these in the sewing supplies section of your local craft store.

Wet Ingredients – The ingredients in a recipe which are wet or damp. Examples include water, eggs, milk and vanilla extract.

FURTHER READING

These are just a few other books you might like to check out of
the library if you enjoyed this book.

The Dangerous Book for Boys by Conn and Hal Iggulden. Published by Harper
Collins, 2006. (A fantastic book that should be in every boy's library.)

The Kids Campfire Book by Jane Drake & Ann Love. Published by Kids Can Press
Ltd., 1996. (Lots of good recipes and ideas for making firestarters.)

*The Little Book of Whittling: Passing the Time on the Trail, on the Porch, and Under
the Stars* by Chris Lubkemann. Published by Fox Chapel Publishing Company, Inc.,
2005. (A fantastically inspiring book on the art and craft of whittling.)

Knotcraft: The Practical and Entertaining Art of Tying Knots by Allan and Paulette
Macfarlan. Published by Dover Publications, 1967. (A great little introduction to the
useful skill of knot tying.)

**There are so many wonderful field guides out there for kids! Here are two
favorites with great pictures for help in your identifications:**

Songbirds by Jonathan P. Latimer and Karen Stray Nolting. Published by Houghton
Mifflin Company, 2000 (This is one of the *Peterson Field Guides for Young
Naturalists*.)

Insects, Spiders and Other Terrestrial Arthropods by George C. McGavin. Published
by Dorling Kindersley Limited, 2002. (This is one in the terrific *DK Smithsonian
Handbooks* series. Plenty of really awesome photos in these books!)

Notes & Ideas:

Notes & Ideas:

Made in the USA
Lexington, KY
24 March 2012